# AS IS

# *AS IS*

FITZROY DELAHAYE

# ACKNOWLEDGEMENTS

I sincerely wish to acknowledge those people who have been invaluable in the creation and production of this book.
My Thanks to: Tanisha Lamont, Hugh Brown, Jason Munroe, Cassandra Reid, Crystal Taylor and Enrico Smikle.

FIRST EDITION
All rights reserved, including the right of reproduction in whole or in part in any form.
Copyright 2013 by Fitzroy Delahaye

Published by Tanisha Lamont
Samfo Plaza. Spaldings
email:tantee26@yahoo.com
ISBN 978-976-95347-1-1

As it is some things in life never change

As it is, some things in life never change but how we deal with them day by day can make the difference and sometimes that is all we need to do.

# About The Author

A photographer by profession Fitzroy Delahaye was born in Kingston, Jamaica. He migrated to England in 1971 and lived there for 17 years.

He returned home in 1988 where he established his studio and has continued writing ever since. His other written works including the collection of short poems The Painted Words of Emotions.

He now lives in Christiana in the cool central parish of Manchester.

# Contents

**CHAPTER 1**
**LOVE**

| | |
|---|---|
| Acknowledgements | ii |
| About the Author | iv |
| Contents | v-vi |
| Preface | vii |
| A LOOK | 1 |
| A Negligible Speck | 1 |
| Afraid | 2 |
| Am I | 3 |
| Beautiful Thing | 4 |
| Because of You | 5 |
| Burnt Letter | 6 |
| Condemned | 7 |
| Easy Come | 8 |
| Gone into Hiding | 9 |
| Heavy Heart | 10 |
| How You Look Today | 11 |
| I Have Nothing | 11 |
| I Surrender | 12 |
| I Want So Much | 12 |
| If Only I Could | 13 |
| Kill the love | 14 |
| Like An Army | 15 |
| Like Me | 16 |
| Like The Dark Clouds | 17 |
| My Desperate Heart | 17 |
| Love And Hate | 18 |
| Married Women | 19 |
| I'm A Psychopath | 20 |
| Not Having You Beside Me | 21 |
| Only A Woman | 22 |
| Sad For Making You So Happy | 22 |
| Stop Moving | 23 |
| Tainted Love, A Thing To Be Avoided | 24 |
| This Year | 24 |
| Take Me | 25 |
| The Joke's On You | 26 |
| The Reverse Is The Same | 27 |
| Your Silence | 28 |
| Were We So Wrong For Each Other? | 28 |
| Wake Up | 29 |
| Why? | 30 |
| She Looks And Look | 30 |
| Voice From The Hills | 31 |
| The Depth Of Your Darkness | 31 |

# Contents

## CHAPTER 2
## PEOPLE AND EMOTIONS

| | |
|---|---|
| A Big House | 34 |
| Clouds | 34 |
| A Little House | 35 |
| Bad Manners | 35 |
| Dawning On Me | 36 |
| False | 37 |
| Family Opinions | 37 |
| Fools | 38 |
| Gifts In A Plastic Bag | 38 |
| Great Men | 39 |
| I Feel Your Pain | 39 |
| Painted | 40 |
| Pride | 40 |
| Resentment | 41 |
| So Fast | 42 |
| Tears | 42 |
| Tears Of Gratitude | 43 |
| The Difference | 43 |
| The Ill Mannered | 44 |
| Up And Down | 44 |
| A Tribute To The Greats | 45 |

## CHAPTER 3
## NATURE AND SEASONS

| | |
|---|---|
| Gilbert '88 | 48 |
| Laying Flat | 49 |
| Sandy's Visit | 49 |
| Wild Gilbert | 50-51 |
| Time | 51 |
| Nature's Role | 52 |
| Silent Whispers | 52 |

## CHAPTER 4
## SOCIAL

| | |
|---|---|
| Reggae Music | 56 |
| Can't Tell | 57 |
| Gods For Fools | 57 |
| Hungry To Be Fooled | 58 |
| Sacrifice | 58 |
| Politics | 59 |
| London Burning | 59 |
| The Real World | 60-61 |
| Senseless | 61 |
| The System | 62 |
| Slaves Of Hate | 62 |

# Preface

This anthology of poems will appeal to all regardless of sex, class and\or opinions. Poetic expressions have been used and loved ever since the existence of time. Lyrics and prose are used in everyday speech, present even if we do not recognize it.

In the putting together of this book I have explored the darker side of LOVE. The journey continued in my interactions with and observations of PEOPLE AND EMOTIONS. SOCIAL commentary came into play with my expressions of the happenings around. My appreciation of NATURE AND SEASONS can be felt here also.

I sincerely hope that you enjoy this book as much as I enjoyed putting it together.

F. Delahaye

# *AS IS*

# CHAPTER 1
# LOVE

## A LOOK

A look of truth and of trust
A look of love and of joy
A look of the pure in heart
A look of songs and of music
A look of connections and Oneness
A look of togetherness
A look of innocent moments
A look of the days and the nights
A look that only you and I could give each other
And fully comprehend
A look of love.

## A Negligible Speck

You can let my love for you be a negligible speck
So don't be afraid of me
Be as free as you want to be
A negligible speck
Can be my love for you only
A negligible speck in your hair can my love be
It cannot stop you
Remember like an eagle you can fly high above my love for you
And then you'll see how negligible this love is
So your days are as they have always been
My loving you need not give you the blues
You're still in control
Calling the shots
As my love for you is a negligible speck
If you so want it to be.

# Afraid

Afraid
Afraid I once was of you,
Of your beauty, your grace,
 Your charm, your face
 Your power, your fame
 But mostly of your rejection.

But now, I am no longer afraid of you, but for you.
For you have found someone else to give your heart to
 Too soon
 Someone who may not love you like I would want you to be loved.
Someone you have found who may love you for the duration of a full moon

Oh I'm afraid for you as you are on an unknown path and only time would tell
If my fear for you is warranted or not; the waiting is hell

# Am I

Am I really so dumb
Am I so blind that I can't see?
That falling in love with you is going to be
 The end of me.
Am I so weak to say no?
 Even though
You are a blazing fire and a raging storm.
Why am I not running away from you?
Knowing you're like fired bullets looking for flesh to rest in.
Why do you have me hypnotized?
Unable to see sense.
Why am I making myself fall in love with you even though
I know
You are a black hole of darkness
A one-way ticket to hell.
Why do I feel so in need of help?
Slipping away from myself
 Into your web of sorrow
Into your world not known to me.
Am I just dreaming? Oh how I wish.
I wish.

# Beautiful Thing

Oh what a beautiful thing love is
Having the force to bond two hearts together
Like that of a mother and child
How does a baby know the power of love?
Enough to give it back to its mother
Why does a child yearn for love?
As essential as food
Love sings so deeply that all can take note
From the hills, from the trees, from the valleys, to the very seas
We can hear the melodies of love
Love smiles in the dark
Love shines in the soul of man in a special way
Love's way
Love has no limits
Like the air that we breathe
Love is bountiful
 Can never run out
Even though it's been around
Since the beginning of time.

# Because of You

Because of you other women have become empty shells to me
So I pass them by without a glance
Because of you I know now what unswerving love is
Because of you
 I've come to know love's powers
Because of you I rise with the sun
And wait around for it to set
Because of you
I now give freely my love
Because of you I now have a yearning for love
Because of you
 I can go insane
Because of you I now know where I belong
Because of you I can say what it is to have fallen in love.
Because of you I can say I know tears of love and joy.
Because of you I can say I know what
it feels like to really care for someone.
Because of you I can see my strengths, my weaknesses and faults.
Because of you I now know what it is to miss someone.
Because of you I now run to the telephone like a race horse.
Because of you I now take the country bus with a delight.
Because of you I can now live with myself.

# Burnt Letter

I burnt the letter that described the way
Your heart used to feel about me
Oh how things can change in the passing of the stream of time
So quickly
Especially love
Love lives today and stops time
Then dies tomorrow and releases at the drop of a dime

I burnt the letter that confirmed that in this life
 You once had in your heart thoughts of you as my wife
I burnt the letter that showed that once upon a time
There was a bridge connecting your heart to mine.

# Condemned

I have been sent to you by a force not known to me before
A force I could not question
A shapeless force called love
Moving so fast in the air
Having me blown into your path causing a stir
I await my fate now in fear
I lie in wait for my sentence
I have been condemned
To be a galley slave?
Face the firing squad?
To be hanged?
Tortured?

Love is not white or black
Female or male
Love is not partial like you and I
Oh in agony I await my fate
A result of being sent to you by love

# Easy Come

Love is easy to form
So hard to keep
We can fall in love everyday
But to stay
In love is a difficult thing
Because love is surrounded by more enemies than friends
Love comes and goes just like the unstable wind
Love can take years to form, years to cherish
Years to grow, years to nourish
And yet so easily, so quickly
Love goes away
Love can be formed just about anywhere
But to keep love, none of these places help
When love is dissipating
Nothing is there to say
Stay

Oh, when love decides to quit
What power it shows, what gloom
What hate it shows to the one who wants to keep it
How painful it can be when it shows it's real self to the one who plays with it
What doom
If you are not ready to keep love in its right place then don't reach for it
Love transforms itself
To find those who misuse it
And then it will repay those who are not it's friends

# Gone into Hiding

You make me feel like I'm a big cat hunting you down day and night
So you've gone into hiding
My phone calls you do not answer as if I would find you
You pass by so silently so I will not hear or see you
You spray the air that I may not breathe you in
So as not to get a clue as to where you are
Out of my sight you stay
So you take the long way to pass me by
Is it my love that you are afraid of?
Or is it your hate for me?
That has been keeping you away
Hide, hide as you may
Hide high
Hide low
My love for you is still growing.

# Heavy Heart

My heart poured like a heavy shower of rain
With emotions of every kind
So heavy was my heart I could not stand up even if I tried
Just could not carry the weight on my own
Did not know I would last to see another day
Yet I could not share…
Could not even let you know
Every time you come near
I fall to the ground
 But you could not see me lying there
Love for you had me crawling….
Begging for mercy
Love for you made me forget that there was a "me"
I was too busy planning for you
Thinking of the things you do
Could not wait to share the space in my heart
Just could not wait to share the space you've owned
 Since you opened my heart and let yourself in.

# How You Look Today

How you looked today made me stare in awe
At your grace
Looking at you, a morning star
When I laid my eyes on you today I saw
A shooting star
So glorious is your beauty today
 Glowing with indignation though as you laid eyes on me
And you glowed also with your usual pride
The radiance of a rainbow is what I am seeing
Looking at you today
Sunrise
Sunbeam
Your beauty truly is

# I Have Nothing

Sometimes, at some point in our lives
We all feel these words said by whitney houston
"I have nothing"
So I "run to you,"
Hoping to find my strength in you.
Don't run away from me, stay that I may
Possess you as my own.
"Don't walk away from me," I want you to be mine always.
Is there no place where my broken heart can go?
I think you are that place,
Where I can find peace, love and understanding.
And "dance with someone who loves me,"
 The greatest gift of my life would be having you beside me
For always.
Indeed what power we can have in the mind, heart and soul
Of another human being when we think we have fallen in love
with them and they with us.

## I Surrender

I just had to surrender to you
Having been blown to pieces by
Your words of wisdom;
This pulled out all the stops in me.
And then plugged me in with all light needed
To show me the way
That I ought to have been going.

I surrender to your motherly advice
 To your wisdom
 To your pleads
Open handedness and love

## I Want So Much

I want so much to know you
I want so much to hear you
I want so much to know why it is that I love you so much
Days and nights I search for answers but you hold the keys
If I could just get you to hear me out
But just for a minute then maybe I would be set free
Free as you who have me under lock and key
Drowning in deep, deep emotions over you
Oh, I want so much to be free
Like you are

# If Only I Could

If only I could
If only I would
If only I can
If only you would just give me a chance to help you I would right now
I would like to reach out and grab you real tight
 And pull you with all my might
From the evil that has you wrapped up in its halls
 Pinning you to invisible walls
Not having a say about when to move and what to do
Is making you so sad, lonely and afraid
If only I could tell you that I know you are being held with a force beyond your understanding
But you can help us
To hear
To feel
 To see
 To taste
To understand what you are going through.

# Kill The Love

I killed the love that was so pure, gentle and sweet
I killed the love that had me caring for you
Feeling your pain
Your sorrow
I killed the love that made me think about your well-fare
Your well-being
I killed the love that moved me to give out of my needs to you
I killed the love that would not have harmed you in any way
I killed the love that was like a mother's love
I killed the love that was one of a kind
 I killed the love that showed how special you are
 I killed the love that made you feel out of place when you see me
 I killed the love that caused you pain and disappointment
I killed the love that had me making plans for you
 I killed the love that had me having regrets
I killed the love that made me into a poet
 I killed the love that should not have been
I killed the love that Adam felt when he laid eyes on Eve
Burst into poetry "This is at last bone of my bones and flesh of my flesh"

# Like An Army

Like an army she surrounded me
Seeking answers to the things that came from my heart
To the tip of my pen
Surrounded indeed, I am by this army-like woman
Wanting confirmation about my love for her
But how could I deny what she already knew
I had to surrender to her

Like an army ready for the attack
A glaze in her eyes fixed to mine
A great rage
Ready to blow me away for having told her of my love for her
My love for her has caused a war indeed
 The cost of love is not always a bed of roses
Indeed the cost of love is sometimes the cause of war.

# Like Me

Like me you were not told about the journey of love
Who it would come from and who you would give it to
Like me you were left all alone to figure it out
Like me you may not be able to
Like me it is going to frighten you
Like me it would blow you to pieces
Like me it would cause a storm
Carrying you high and low
Like me you'll ask "who gave you the right to fall in love with me?"
"Shame on you
You could be my father
I am disappointed
Leave me alone you are a psychopath!"
Like me you think this cannot be happening
Like me you did not know that love is a miracle
Like the birth of a baby who did not ask to be born
Who did not choose it's parents
Its color
Its sex
It's time or place of birth
Like me you did not choose who to fall in love with
Whether poor or rich
Younger or older
White or black

Like me you can be forced to kill the love before it is born
Like me you will fall in love with the wrong person
The wrong person with you.

# Like The Dark Clouds

Like the dark clouds hovering over the hills of Christiana on a late Sunday evening
Without the company of the sun rays. Birds glide by with a song
Cheering the dawn of night, As they say goodbye to another day.
Like the dark clouds standing
Still wondering where to go next So are my feelings for you. Like the dark clouds so lonely and blue Is the heaviness of my heart since losing you.

Like the dark clouds having to wait for the turning of the sun
I am waiting for you to turn me around.
Make me the opposite of what I am now
Like a smile to a frown.

# My Desperate Heart

My desperate heart makes me want you so badly
Even though danger is written all over you
Danger of disaster
Of heartache
Of pain
Of sadness and of fear
Danger of love and loneliness
Danger of my own death, to an early grave
My desperate heart yearns to hear your voice
See your face
Feel your presence and your touch
My desperate heart beats a thousand times faster when I think of you
My desperate heart makes me feel so vulnerable because of you.

# Love And Hate

Feelings of deep affection
 Fondness,
And great liking is what you receive from me
Dislike and hate is what I get from you
Love and hate
Love and hate keeps us apart
I love you
You hate me
My love, your hate causes a spark that keeps us apart
The more I feel your hate the safer I become in the space that we share
The more you hear of my love for you the more you despise me
Love and hate keeps us where we belong
Apart from each other
I am afraid to let go of your hate for me
As you may make a switch and turn love and hate into one and then we'll both sink to the bottom.
Love and hate keeps us floating to see another day.

# Married Women

I am afraid so afraid of the touch of a married woman
I am afraid of the smile of a married woman
I am afraid of the voice of a married woman
I am afraid of the handshake of a married woman

I am afraid of the eye contact of a married woman
I am afraid of the offer of a car ride from a married woman
I am afraid of the house of a married woman
I am afraid of the tears of a married woman

I am afraid of the sadness of a married woman
I am afraid of the loneliness of a married woman
I am afraid of the cries of a married woman
I am afraid of the complaints of a married woman

I am afraid of the charm of a married woman
I am afraid of the grace of a married woman
I am afraid of the beauty of a married woman
I am afraid of the embrace of a married woman

I am afraid of the love of a married woman
I am afraid of being captured in a world where I do not belong
A world without return.

# I'm A Psychopath

I'm a psychopath for caring about you
For making plans for you
I'm a psychopath for seeing how beautiful you really are
I'm a psychopath for noticing how strong and brave you are
And for wanting to give a helping hand to you
I'm a psycho for sharing your dreams, hopes and your plans
I'm a psycho for wanting you to continue
Burning like a candle with hope in the wind
I'm a psycho for being inspired by your words of truth
Your charm
Your humor
Why do you not think a normal guy like me could fall in love with you?
Why must it be a psycho that could have told you
Of the invisible force that you possess
Why must it be a psycho to have rolled over and over?
 Just to get your attention
Because of the power you possess you would have even kings eating out of your hands
Like the psycho I have become because of you

# Not Having You Beside Me

Feeling so lonesome not having you beside me,
To hold so gently
Whisper things you like to hear.
 I feel so distant and alone
That I just had to hear your voice
That I just want to let you know
that`s why I called so late
I know hearing your voice
Will let me see the dawn of the day
So that I may
Carry on without you by my side
Oh I wish I wasn't so far away from you
Hearing just your voice is not enough
But I know that is all I can have for now
Until I return into your arms
 I will squeeze you so tightly
As if there will be no tomorrow.

# Only A Woman

Only a woman makes me feel feelings never known to me before.
Only a woman makes me feel brave and so fearful at the same time.
Only a woman can touch parts of me I did not know.
Only a woman can show me all the beauty that the world possesses in one second.

Only a woman can sing melodies with just a smile.
Only a woman can make me travel through space at the speed of light.
Only a woman can make me want to dream Dreams over and over again.
Only a woman can make me feel complete.

Only a woman can love me to death without a trace.
Only a woman can carry my child unto planet earth.

# Sad For Making You So Happy

Sad for making you so happy when I know I can never be yours
Sad for making you so happy when I can only be loaned to you
Happy you are in my presence I know
 You get a thrill
 You glow as the morning sun
Sad for making you so happy when I cannot bring you forward
As my own
Happy you are today as you are with me
The moments we spend together now cause you to forget
Tomorrow and the pain it may bring
Sad for making you so happy,
When sadness is at the end for you and I.

# Stop Moving

Moving
Moving so much
Moving
 Searching for a space to call your own
A space where you belong
A space where you can sleep in peace
 Dream as you will
Until you stop moving you will not be able to see
What it is you're looking for
As even the moving leaves stop at some point
 Become productive
Why don't you start today?
Stop running away from yourself
Let me help you to see the gem that I see in you
All the reasons to believe in you
Fall in love with you
Let me share the love I have for you
 So you can share it with yourself too.

# Tainted Love, A Thing To Be Avoided

Gone blind,
 Deaf,
Dumb all at once
After seeing me or so it seems as you played
Why should love cause you to behave so strangely?
Is it such an alien thing for you?
I saw you dash across to the other side when you beheld me
Hoping the ground would just open up and take you in
Why should love be doing this to you?
Or is it because it is one-sided
Why should something so beautiful,
 So miraculous
Be causing such a rift between you and I.

# This Year

Why do l crumble because of you?
When I have only known you for a week
Curtailed I feel
Curtailed is my every move because of you
Dazzling to me are the many expressions
Crawling over your face
 Some of sadness
Seeming to be begging for mercy
Darling oh darling
My heart wants you to be my darling
Even if this year for me
Be it that it may be
The death of me.
Fearful I feel of 2013.

# Take Me

I yearn for the day to come when you will be mine
The day when we will make known to the world that it is time
When we will make the solemn vow on our wedding day before our special guests
 Who would include angels from the four corners of the heavens to bear witness

To the love that has yoked us together on this our wedding day.
When the day will have moved on to give way to the silence of the night when I will say
 Take me, feather me with the clouds of your love, and rock me
With the charm that graces you so tenderly

Sing to me the song that only you have from the stars of the heavens above
Shelter me with the strength that you possess
Kiss me with the eye of your heart and cuddle me with your every breath.
  So I can meet the rising sun a million miles away and become the owner of your love.

# The Joke's On You

They are laughing
They are joking
They are talking because the joke is on you
I am crying for you because I know what is going on with you
 It is no joke
So sad I become when I hear your name coming from their mouths
So sad I become when I hear their thoughts with you in their minds

A little girl you are I know crying out for help
Crying out of pain
No one hears you
No one sees your tears running down your face
Like blood from your veins
Only a face wearing a frown they see
Only a voice echoing hate they hear
Only a girl acting strange coming their way
No one wants to see the cause but only the joke that is on you.

# The Reverse Is The Same

Falling in love can be so devastating
Just like falling out of love.
Love is not a one way street, not always a bed of roses
Falling in love can keep you from sleeping
Like falling out of love
Falling in love can make you so afraid of the known and the unknown
Likewise falling out of love
Falling in love is like landing on the moon
Without knowing how you got there in the first place
Falling out of love can send you to a never-ending low
Falling in love causes you to ask a thousand and more questions
Without answers
So like falling out of love
Like me, like you falling in love will curb freedom
Falling out of love is setting me free
Daily we are forced to make a choice.

# Your Silence

The silence that you give
The silence that you give is just too much for me to carry
Just too loud for me to deal with
The silence I get from you makes the dropping of a pin
Seem as an explosion in my ear
The silence from you is just too much to carry
It has blackened my days
Leaving me so afraid to meet the starless nights
I must be under your spell
While you've taken some space not to be heard from or be seen
Yet I cannot stop searching listening out for you
I must be under your spell
The reason why I suffer so much in silence
Is you.

# Were We So Wrong For Each Other?

Having being together for ten years
 You decided to leave me.
It's been a week since you've been gone
 Without a word, without a trace
Yet it doesn't grieve me
I do not miss you
Is it because we were so wrong
For each other why I now feel so free?
Gone out of my sight, and out of my hearing
You have gone out of my life
I am set free.

# Wake Up

Back off
Get real
Wake up
It won't work
She's not ready for your kind of love
She's ice-cold
You are red hot
A world apart she is from you
Leave her
Let her be
Try as you may there is no way you can win her love for you
You cannot tame her
Get real, back off
Kill the volcano inside you
That has been erupting inside your heart since you've known her
Iceberg
Glacier
Ice-sheet
That is what you are up against
No way you can win her over with your volcanic love.

# Why?

Why don't you shine like the star that you are?
The brightest star in the sky, is you
Yet you are not shining as you should
Why oh why don't you glow
Is it too dark where you are?
Then why don't you make a break
 Come into my space where I will make you shine like the bright star that you are
Why should you stay where you don't belong?
In the dark
You are the bright star remember
You need to shine
So get out from the dark so that you will be able to shine
 Like the bright star that you are.

# She Looks And Look

She keeps on looking and she looks and looks again She keeps on looking and she looks and looks again Then she begins to stare Staring her way out of everything taking place around her What is she looking at so much? Her young baby who seem to have taken her over into another world, another place, another time What magnet her baby has now become to her She now breathe feel and touch This child, that has now become her world. Because she has given birth to it It has turned her upside down No more can she ever become free of motherhood
Fear not felt before has become part of her Voice not heard before she will now hear Joy not felt before, she will now feel Love not known before has now taken her over.

# Voice From The Hills

I heard your voice rolling down from the hill As it echoed through the trees with total charm and grace To fill the air of my heart Oh how the trees danced to your voice As it made connection with mine for the first time You smiled from the hills Lighting up the surroundings and my heart all at once
I hear your voice
I still hear it singing through my soul Could it be the voice I used to hear? When I was a fetus in the womb of my mother? Could your voice be the one? I waited a thousand full moons for And climbed all the hills and mountains In Jamaica in search of?
Yes it must be, as I now feel so complete.

# The Depth Of Your Darkness

Why are you so dark, sullen and angry? A dark mood covers your every move. When I see you I see the dark ages being driven back in time, with you by my side. Oh what a fright I sooner died than being with you. Your anger causes even the invisible air to shiver and vibrate. Dark and sullen to the core you are. You seem so fixed in the dark, even the sunshine does not make you budge. And like others before me I too have to take my leave. Dark, sullen angry, a dark mood hovering over you is what you seem to know. Are you so tightly clad in this robe of darkness that you cannot even budge an inch? Your darkness is too much for me, yet I still love you.

# CHAPTER 2
# PEOPLE AND EMOTIONS

# A Big House

A big house with everything
Enough room for everyone
Furnished to everyone's comfort
A big house to get away from each other

Love is nowhere to be found
In that home
As each one seeks his own
Each One runs underground

No one wants to head home in a rush
There is no love to run to there
So lonely is this big house lacking love's touch
So empty of joy and the sound of laughter and care

 No happiness within these walls
Wives hide away in guest rooms
To shed tears for yesterday, today and tomorrow
Knowing everything resides here
 Except love

# Clouds

Clouds, Clouds
Everyone will one day face their clouds
Black cloud of despair
Black cloud of disappointments
Black cloud of fear
Black cloud of pain
Black cloud of sickness
Black cloud of death
Everyone will have to face their day of black cloud.

# A Little House

A little house
 A big family
Sharing everything
Laughter
Joy
Sorrow
Pain
A little house where everyone wants to be
Even though everything has to be shared

We did not mind because we had love to bind us together
We knew the secret of sharing our home
Home sweet home
Each other
As love permeated our walls and held us together.
Cherish the moments.

# Bad Manners

Bad Manners has taken over our land
 Our people are not able to behave mannerly anymore
As good manners have taken a hike
Bad manners have become no problem
Cool running's our new motto.
As it is the norm nobody seems to notice that bad manners is out of place
Children are taught only bad manners so what else can we expect from our people
But cool runnings
Bad manners is the in thing.

# Dawning On Me

Dawning on me - in a crowd of a thousand and more
Is this situation that I am in?
Being unable to stop the tears flowing from my core
As I reflect on the way things really are
 Flowing tears to ease the pain at the thought of being alone.
Even in a crowd of a thousand and more
 No one hears
No one sees
Oh how I wish my mother - the cause of my pain and tears - could see.
Me
In a crowd of a thousand and more
Wasting away in full view of her
My mother
Who sees me not?
 Hears me not
And feels me not.
And I do not know why
It makes me cry
In a crowd of thousands
 Even more.

# False

It's hard to determine what's real from what is not
As everything is so false
False nail
False teeth
False eyes
False hair
False skin
False friends
False breasts
False witnesses
False doctors
False pharmacist
False police
False music.

# Family Opinions

So strong
So deep
So wide
So powerful are the opinions of my family
That I have not been able to show to them the love of my heart
The love of my life
So afraid of what I may hear them say about the one that I love
I just keep him away
We take a hike out of their sight
We take a flight out of their sight

# Fools

Fools have taken over the place,
 Foolish are the sounds they are making
Foolish are the things they are doing
 To themselves and to others
Fool's paradise is what the land has become
 As a result of the empty-headed
The island is so saturated with foolish people
That there is just no light in sight
The land is blanketed with fools

# Gifts In A Plastic Bag

Gifts in a plastic bag I receive daily
From a little golden girl
Who knows how to give what she has
 Gifts in a plastic bag I receive gladly
 Because I know it is coming from a heart of love

Gifts in a plastic bag have been handed to me
Even in a crowd of many
By this little golden girl of love

Gifts in a plastic bag from this girl
Has taught me the meaning of giving
Gifts in a plastic bag have helped to form a bond
Of love between me and this little golden girl
That will never end while I'm living.

# Great Men

News of the death of great men grips me with fear,
Not of my own death,
But of my own life.
News of the death of great men shows the folly of wanting to be great.

Great men are only great in the minds of those who forget,
Those so called great men will die.
Great men are normally recognized as being really great,
When they die.

# I Feel Your Pain

I feel your pain, your distress, your suffering
Expression of a pained soul I see when I look at you
I feel your pain deep inside of me choking me to death
By feeling your pain my days are black and blue
Your pain has become mine too
And why I do not know
I hear your pain in your words
Your voice, your sighs, and your silence
I see your pain in your every move
In your walking and sitting down
I see your pain watching you laying down in them
Covering you over like a blanket
I smell your pain when you enter my thoughts
I taste your pain in a way never before felt
I am touched by your pain all over
I am so consumed by them
I am indebted to you for me becoming a better person.

# Painted

You have painted me so heavily
With your pains and sorrows
So wet I am now since being in contact with you
Unable to be dried
Like the gloom of winter, are the colors you have me painted with
Your tears of pain have painted your face away from what it used to be
A coat of fear has now taken you over
 The color of hope is all I have to give to you
To wash your blues away

# Pride

For some, pride has taken a dive from its elevated state
Achievements used to be its crown to its credit
Self-respect used to be the aim
Now high opinion of self is the rule
Good appearance has taken a back seat
Anything goes
Wherever the breeze blows
Where behavior is concerned
Women's breasts half-bared in the face
Other body parts have 'for sale' written all over
As for their heads you see a scarecrow
Signaling that a mirror has been used back to front
As for their faces you see a clown without the nose
Now as for their counterpart
They wear their trousers from their knees down
 A style that was once seen on women has now become theirs
As women no longer show their hair
They now use a mask
Counterparts of women are now able to compete with them in just about anything
As pride is no longer present in an unproud world

# Resentment

Old and frail
Messy and stupid
Out of touch with everything
Talking rubbish unceasingly
Ill-mannered
Dependent
This is the condition a man turned up in my life in
Revealing himself to me
As my father
My kin
When I was a child he was nowhere to be found
He took himself out of my life
When I needed him the most he was not there
I would have suffocated if he was my air
How I ate he did not know
Did not provide my clothes, gave no shoe
If I was alive or dead he had no clue
Now I've become a man not needing him
He shows up to be dependent on me
I, who was never given the chance to be dependent on him,
Oh resentment is killing me.

# So Fast

So fast she went away
So fast she left us
Without a chance to say goodbye
So fast you pulled away from the evil force that took you over
So fast you took your leave from what would have become for you
A torture chamber
Had you not left as fast as you did things would have ended?
 But not in your favor

So fast you moved away so no one could've taken pity on you
As we all did with your sister who went before you
So ravished by the same evil force
The force of Cancer.

So fast you went out of this life
We are left pondering the fate of our own.

# Tears

Tears, tears,
Tears of fear.
Tears of pain
Tears of sorrow
Tears of desperation
Tears like hail from her face.

Tears
 Crying for mercy
Waiting for the rising sun to dry them away
Tears from women blow the strength of men away
Leaving them standing so alone and vulnerable.

# Tears Of Gratitude

Tears of gratitude flow out of me
So heavily
Because of what you have been doing for me.
Even though I did not ask you to be my maid
You have chosen to do so for me
You have seen my need so you have come to my rescue.
And all that I was able to give to you
Were hugs and wet kisses in return
Tears of gratitude flow
So heavily
In my sleep
In my dreams
I just had to wake up only to find you are gone.

# The Difference

They run,
You stay,
They say,
You do.
They promised, you fulfilled,
They break, you build.
They discourage, you encourage.

This is the difference between a mother's love
And that of men.
Men seem to be everything that they are not,
But you mom, are everything
That I need to pull me through life.
Everything I've got.

# The Ill Mannered

You see them every day
You hear them day and night,
They are well-dressed; drive the best vehicles, in the best jobs,
They go to the best schools so you would expect better from them
You stop your vehicle for them to cross the road and they do not say thanks
You hold the door for them and you become invisible in their sight
They don't acknowledge you in any way
They talk so loudly on their phones
Any place they please
You would think they own the world
The ill mannered need to be cured.

# Up And Down

Up and down
Up and down beyond my will
Like a bouncing ball out of control
I go up and down
Paying the price for being high and low
Driving away the few friends I know
Because I am bipolar.

# A Tribute To The Greats

A tribute, a tribute to the great
What can I contribute to these great men and women?
Who once stood so tall, formidable?
Now they crumble like Jericho's wall
They are now so weak and feeble
To rise up they are unable

What can I contribute but pity?
    A Pity for what I now see,
    A Pity for what I now hear
    A pity for what I now feel
    A pity for what I now know
Great they were when they were young,
But now they have become too much like
Normal men and women
Old and gray and weak
No longer bold
Moving ever closer to their end.
An end that I am afraid to meet,
But like them I now know that I will
I have to greet that end.

# CHAPTER 3
# NATURE AND SEASONS

# Gilbert '88

Why did you blow away so many things from our land?
Singing voices can no longer be heard since you flew by
The long hair of ladies are no more seen blowing from side to side
With a shine so captivating to the eyes
So as to cause a stare
Caught up in the fray
Garments in disarray
Breasts are no longer hidden out of sight
As are the empty backsides that go bare since you flew by
Before you flew by
Body parts were concealed
From men who had no right to see
What they did not pay the price
By a commitment to see
Men's vice
Blown away
Nothing to cover bulges that would normally be seen only
By that special one
Music, sweet music that is used to heal the soul is no more
Has gotten blown out of ears
You have blown in fear
Songs that use to fill the air with love,
Hope and dreams have been removed
Manners has deserted people completely
Car horns have been blown away
Left around the corner
No more do our drivers make a sound as they drive
As fast as when you flew by
Eye sights seem to be failing
As everyone that drives seem to be shortsighted
As they only seem to apply their brakes in the process of an impact.

# Laying Flat

Laying flat, so flat and straight
So blue, so calm
With countless ripples, moving so orderly
Like the golden waltz
Without a wave in sight
To disturb the compactness of your ripples
A still blueness that seems to be so endless
So congealed
Trillions of trillions of gallons
One body of blueness
Known as the Caribbean Sea

# Sandy's Visit

Sandy's visit caused quite a stir on our little island
She caused free rides on the highway
Caused my bed to rise like the waters she brought
Removed all the sporting activities from the land
Caused JPS to cut their power,
 Leaving us high and dry in darkness
Sandy caused a complete shut-down in Jamaica
 She reigned as a queen on the land
The trees danced to her song, to her music
Some to their deaths
The rivers and the gullies rose in her honor
The sea transported her in all her glory and power
The inhabitants of the land ran and hid in fear
When they heard Sandy was near.

# Wild Gilbert

The full impact of your visit over our land is now being seen and felt
As your deadly force not only removed what was in your path so you could pass by
But also to open the way for what you had carried with you
Like the heavy showers that you had brought
The devastation you wrought
So is the number of mobile phones
That passed the patios along the airwaves to different homes
As you did with frightening speeds and sounds
Like the deadly missiles you blew all through the air
 So is the number of cans you carried over here
Like the wide path you took on your journey
So are the highways you have given us
Like the debris you brought along when you visited
Are the wigs
And panties
That bared heads and bottoms
Just as you bared trees you battered and shook
Guns and bullets
Like the zinc and nails
You sent flying with deadly force
Ready to maim anyone in the way
Drugs
Like the many poisoned waters that run from the gullies
 That you brought back to life
Violence
 Which you used on the millions of uprooted trees
 Cut down by the force you unleashed upon them

Computers
Like the graphic colors you gave the clouds
 Before you made your dissent and had us hearing and seeing strange things
Dances
 Like the lovemaking you beheld when you removed the roofs
And got a view of the inside happenings
Gyrations
Twisting and turning
Like you had the trees doing when you had your eye fixed on them

# Time

Time gives and takes away
Time gives life and time takes life away.
Time give joys, sadness and tears
Times gives health and strength
 And then takes them back again.
Time is the past, present and future.
Time is the master,
 Reigning today tomorrow and forever.

# Nature's Role

The clouds blanket the trees to keep them warm
The rain sends the trees to sleep
The breeze causes the trees to sing
The sun causes the trees to grow and bear fruit
The moon causes the trees to dream
The stars causes the trees to dance in the dark,
Human cause the trees to die.

# Silent Whispers

The silent whispers of the night
Creatures
Singing their songs of praise
To the one who made them all.

Oh what lovely sounds they are making
Oh with their songs, how can the night be silent?
Oh with their songs, the blind will know the night
Oh with their songs who can but take notice

So many nocturnal creatures singing their songs
And yet who can say "I cannot sleep"
Because of this nightly chorus
The invisible singers of the night
Makes us aware of the nights teeming creatures.

# CHAPTER 4 SOCIAL

# Reggae Music

Reggae
Reggae music
So magnetically reaching
Reaching right into the heart
Into the souls of men.
Reggae power causes heads to rock from side to side.
The Reggae beat come with a force no man can resist.
Reggae rhythm has even white people rocking to its sweet sugary sound.
Reggae music is the sound of us, the people,
We the Jamaicans, talking to the world.
It speaks for us all.
Rise people to the sound of reggae music.
To the beat that says all men are equal
All have rhythmic character implanted in their souls.
Reggae
Reggae Rhythm
Reggae Power
Reggae Beat blows away the problems facing us.
This music is redemption for all.
To the four corners of the earth
Reggae vibration is being felt.
So strong it causes a response from a fetus inside a womb.
Reggae
Reggae music lives on.

# Can't Tell

Can't tell anymore what's right from wrong
Fools sound like the sane
The sane behave like the insane
In the way of dress and in words
Gays look like the "straight"
"Straight" look like Gays
Whores fit in just about anyplace
As every other woman dresses like a whore
Black women look like brown women
 After killing their skin
Poisoning it
Heads are now covered with alien hairstyles
You would think you're in India
Skin branded all over
You would think you are in a slaughterhouse
Viewing tested meat
Or branded cattle.

# Gods For Fools

Flocked together with their followers shouting for them
Whining for them
Thinking for them,
Jumping for them
Gods for fools set the trends in dressing
Talking, dancing and in behavior
Gods for fools have poisoned the minds of our young ones
With their music and lifestyles
Gods for fools is getting younger by the day
Gods for fools run the airwaves and the dancehall
Gods for fools are in control.

# Hungry To Be Fooled

Moving through the air with a wind -forced breeze
In droves from towering hills and the deep valley
Saturating cities and town to hear empty promises of every kind
Men's folly
Soaking up every word like rain drops on dessert sand
Like gullible children waiting for ice cream from baby cows
Candy from a babe's hand
Blowing all at once in the same direction
To hear once again what they had heard
Not so long ago but which they seem to have forgotten
They cling to every word
Oh so hungry they are to be fooled again
 And again.

# Sacrifice

Falling from the face
Without grace
Blood and tears
Given to the Gods of the land
Sacrifice
The more they get the more they want
So today my blood has been
Taken with my tears
The tears of my loved ones
 Tomorrow it could be yours
The Gods of violence want more and more
Blood and tears
Blood and tears pave a one-way street on my face
An unending stream
Blood and tears staring you in the face

# Politics

All hell breaks loose
Cars, vans and trucks fly by with lightning speed
Horns blare
Voices rise
 Music thumps
Pots clang
On city streets noises raised to the highest level
Crowded vehicles
With orange and green clad bodies sticking out of windows.
Rush by with rocket speed to their political meetings.
Flags fly in unison born of total madness
Terrors
Excitement
 Clear the way
 Fervor in the air
 Keeping the faint hearted away
 It is election time Jamaican style.

# London Burning

London burning
Burning with fear and tension
Burning with hate
Burning with despair
Burning with violence
Burning with disappointment
Burning with flame
Burning without hope
London burns with problems like the rest of the world.

# THE REAL WORLD

The real world
Many see the real world as a great exciting place
With lots of loving things to do
And they are right
But is our world really as lovely as it seems?
The fact is no.
The real world is not as so many portray it to be.
The real world is hard to take,
So some of us pretend that the real world is just right,
And there are no problems that we cannot handle.
But the real facts remain about the real world in which we live.
Our hospitals aree full of people that are suffering
from one thing or another
And so are our prisons and schools.
Yes the real world is full of people unable to help themselves. Our world is full of sadness and tears,
Pains and sorrow, sickness and death.
We are surrounded by everything but a perfect world.
A world where we can walk the streets without fear,
A world where we can do without our hospitals,
A world where we can say there is no graveyards anymore
A world where we can feel the joys of youth
Even at the age of a thousand years.
A world that is as it seems.
The real world can cause us all to pluck our real feelings;
Our love, our hopes, our joys, our plans and our dreams.
The real world is causing us to become unfeeling,
Unkind, selfish, unloving.
The real world is causing our children to become hopeless,
Helpless, faithless and even lifeless.

Indeed the real world is telling us all to open up our eyes.
And look elsewhere for a relief
Because we cannot go on like this anymore.
We cannot do ourselves any good being on this present course,
A course of selfreliance, a course of self government.
The course of self-destruction.
The world is shouting out ever so loud.

"Change course. Look to the one who put us here for directions,
Because that is the only way out of our problems.
The only way out of a world that shouldn't be.

# Senseless

Gone blind, deaf and dumb at the same time
Gone blind, deaf and dumb all over
No more can a leader be found
All have fallen into the same pit of darkness
All are now so senseless that anything goes
Children lead the way
Doing whatever they may
Because there is no one there to show
Tell them the way to go
Guns bark
Bullets bite into anyone in their path
Tearing away their lives
No one sees as they are blind
No one seems to hear as they are too deaf
No one utters a word as they are so dumb
Gone blind, deaf and dumb all at once

# The System

Crumbling system
Failing its youths
Giving them no hope for today tomorrow and beyond
A crumbled system breeds restless people
Going from side to side
Without a set course to guide them
Crumbling system cries out but to no avail
As no one has the answer for the splinters
Children go to classes
Students go to college
Some get to university
At the end crumbled system has no place for them all
So some turn into pieces
Waiting to be crumbled further by a crumbling system

# Slaves Of Hate

Slaves of hate working so hard
carrying out to space even more hate
Hate in the days right through the nights
Slaves of hate wearing it on the face
Singing it in their songs
slaves of hate carrying it to school
work
and play
slaves of hate are on the increase
Feasting on hate, fattening in the face
Slaves of hate are spreading throughout the land
Slaves of hate are getting younger by the day
Slaves of hate are sending more to the grave

# AS IS

FITZROY DELAHAYE

www.ingramcontent.com/pod-product-compliance
Lightning Source LLC
Chambersburg PA
CBHW021024090426
42738CB00007B/901